# Maggie does Rocket Science

She makes robots that go to space
To take a look at Mars,
And instruments like telescopes
To see beyond the stars.
At school she really liked science,
Her interests were diverse,
And now all that she wants to do is
Tour the universe.

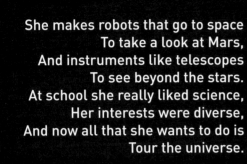

The satellites she makes have shown
How our climate is changing,
Experiments have shown the earth needs us
To start behaving.
We all know that the time is now
But Maggie won't give in,
Maggie Aderin wants to know
When did this time begin?

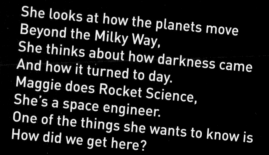

She looks at how the planets move
Beyond the Milky Way,
She thinks about how darkness came
And how it turned to day.
Maggie does Rocket Science,
She's a space engineer.
One of the things she wants to know is
How did we get here?

Now Maggie has gone on a mission,
She wants it to be known
That science is really amazing
As experiments have now shown.
Maggie could have been a bus driver,
A dentist, a chef or a nurse,
But all that Maggie wants to do is
Tour the universe.

# Michelle is a Vet

**Dr Michelle Trebeck** has always loved animals. When she was a child she knew she wanted to work with animals when she grew up. She treats animals of all sizes from fish to horses. The hardest part of her job is getting a cat to go on a diet and take exercise, and making people realise that it is very unhealthy for their pets to be obese.

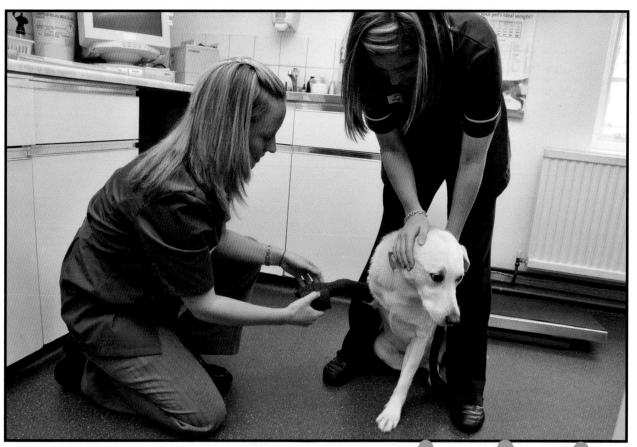

# When I Grow Up

Poems by
**Benjamin Zephaniah**

Photographs by
**Prodeepta Das**

**F**

FRANCES LINCOLN
CHILDREN'S BOOKS

# Maggie is a Rocket Scientist

**Dr Maggie Aderin-Pocock**
was born in London to Nigerian parents. She always wanted to be a scientist, ever since she was a child. She loved science at school, and went on to study Physics at university, and did her Ph D in Mechanical Engineering. She has been behind a number of important inventions, including a hand-held mine detector, a spectograph for calculating the movement of heavenly bodies and a replacement for the Hubble Space Telescope. She is keen to encourage children to be interested in science.

# A Vet for Your Pet

Michelle is a vet,
She can fix your pet
If your pet is dizzy or ill.

If your dog is dodgy
Or your snake is sloppy
Michelle can fix it with a pill.

If your kangaroo
Won't do what they do
Michelle has a sweet sugar lump.

Then your kangaroo
Will go loopy loo
And your kangaroo will just jump.

Michelle is a vet,
She can fix your pet
If your pet will not eat its food.

She'll get out some love
And give it a rub
And your pet will soon change its mood.

If you have two fish
That no longer kiss,
Give our vet Michelle a short time.

Then just as you wish
They'll get quite peckish
And your fish will soon be just fine.

Michelle is a vet,
She'll fix up your pet
If your pet won't go for a walk.

If you have a bird
That won't say a word,
Michelle has ways to help it talk.

If a Nile Crocodile
Has lost its sweet smile
And looks like it's suffering grief,

She'll raise the profile
Of the thick-skinned reptile
And soon it will show you its teeth.

So our vet Michelle
Makes animals well
When they're feeling under the weather.

With tablets and gels
And things with strange smells
She puts hurting creatures together.

Lions will roar
And swallows will soar
And lovebirds will all want to marry.

There's one thing for sure,
Michelle will work more
To make all the animals happy.

# Every Day Away

Every day Ness flies away
Beyond the big white cloud,
Beyond the big white rainmaker,
To Zambia and Jamaica
And way beyond the equator,
In a jumbo jet with a crowd.

Every day Ness flies away
Over the deep blue ocean.
She talks to friends by radio
As she flies over Borneo,
And soon she'll fly to Mexico
With her jumbo jet in motion.

Every day Ness flies away,
Speeding through the sky.
Up there the views are beautiful
And mountains look incredible.
From earth it looks quite magical,
As the plane goes floating by.

Every day Ness flies away,
A plane at her command.
Her passengers are excited,
People who wait are delighted,
For soon they will be united
When Ness brings her plane to land.

# Ness ✈ is a Pilot

**Ness Ovens** is a jumbo jet pilot who has worked with British Airways for 11 years. As a child she was fascinated by aeroplanes in the sky and longed to fly them. After university she was lucky to be accepted on a BA training programme and was taken on by the airline when she graduated. Her husband is also a jumbo pilot and they both fly long-distance. They make sure that at least one of them is at home to look after their two small children. The longest time either is away from home is five days. She loves seeing the earth from high above, especially sunsets over mountains in Africa.

# **Andrew** is a Forest Keeper

**Andrew Gammie** is a senior forest keeper in Epping Forest. He grew up in Warwickshire, on a country estate where his father was a forester. His first school was in a village two miles away, where there were only thirteen children. Andrew wanted to be a vet, but ended up studying art. He started off making props for theatre and film sets. But then he wanted to go back to being amidst nature, and took up a job at Dulwich Park. For the past seven years he has been with Epping Forest, which is owned by the City of London, and has a large deer herd. It is a preserved forest and not a managed forest. This means all trees and natural life are allowed to grow and die naturally. When a storm brings trees down, they are left to decompose instead of being cut into logs and put to use. He likes helping people to enjoy the space and nature of Epping Forest.

# Naturally

He wakes up in the morning as owls return home,
And the leaves come awake to the sun,
He prepares for the day breathing in sweet fresh air
And considers the work to be done.
He's a man of the soil, in love with the earth,
A seeker of true harmony,
He takes care of the forest for you and me
So the forest can thrive naturally.

The animals know him, they see him each day,
Even birds that are high in the sky,
Rabbits and squirrels, herons and deer
Watch him keenly as he passes by.
He's a man of the land, hard-working and
Outdoors is where he wants to be,
He takes care of the forest for you and me
So the forest can thrive naturally.

As well as the animals that call this place home
He also takes care of the trees,
They too can suffer from damage and stress,
Even they can suffer from disease.
He's a man who cares, a man who is there,
A lover of diversity,
He takes care of the forest for you and me
So the forest can thrive naturally.

It's not all about animals, small plants and trees,
It's not all about water and land,
Much of the day is spent talking away
Because human beings too need a hand.
Come wind, rain, or snow, he's ready to go,
A great forest keeper is he,
Taking care of the forest for you and me
So the forest can thrive naturally.

# is a Fashion Designer

**Zandra Rhodes** is one of the top fashion designers in the world, and divides her time between California and London, where she set up The Fashion and Textile Museum, which runs workshops for children. As a child she was inspired by her mother to draw and paint, and grew up to design clothes for many famous people. Her favourite colour is bright pink.

# Style and Fashion

It's all about colour
It's all about flow,
It's all about get up
It's all about go,
It's all about figures
It's all about passion,
It's all about features
It's all about fashion.

It's all about the clothes that we wear every day
Also about the clothes that we wear when we play.

It's all about the dresses
It's all about the shirts,
It's all about the hats and
It's all about the skirts,
It's all about the fit
It's about the versatile,
It's all about the art and
It's all about the style.

It's all about the clothes that we wear to be cool
It's all about the clothes that we wear to school.

It's all about the jackets
It's all about the flair,
It's all about the coats and
It's all about the hair,
It's all about seasons
It's designs from a book,
It's all about the patterns
It's about the way we look.

It's all about the clothes she makes while we wait
It's all about the clothes that she makes that are great.

# Bubblz is a Maths Clown

**Bubblz** wanted to be an engineer like her dad, or a ballet dancer, a hairdresser, a singer or an actress. But she always loved clowns, and her favourite was Charlie Rivel at Circo Price in Madrid, where she grew up. Much later in life, only after she had sold an item on ebay to a clown, she resolved to be a clown herself. Nowadays she visits schools in the UK and abroad, enthusing children about mathematics through her performances.

# Clowning Around

Once upon a time there was a girl called Bubblz
Who had hair that was brown, and long,
She had dreams of becoming a famous singer
To make the world smile with her song.
Once upon a time she tried singing in school
In assembly one Monday morning,
But her voice was so bad, many kids just went mad
And the teachers and cats started yawning.

Then there was a time when this girl called Bubblz
Who had hair that went right down her back,
Wanted to become an actress,
But the problem was she couldn't act.
She starred in a play at the Theatre Royal
A spy thriller set in Shanghai,
But then our girl Bubblz and the whole town knew
That she couldn't act like a spy.

Then on another time this young schoolgirl
Who had hair that most angels admired,
Tried to become a great ballet dancer,
She tried but then soon she retired.
When pirouetting she did too much sweating
And she could not move on her toes,
She twisted and turned, got herself in a whirl
And fell over and damaged her nose.

But this energetic and funny young lady
Did not let all this get her down,
People laughed at her, and that's when she said,
`I knew it all the time, I'm a clown.'
She picked herself up, dusted herself off
And she did a strange dance to a tune.
She counted to ten, she breathed in and then
She blew up a great big balloon.

This young girl has grown and is now a real clown
Who travels from school to school,
Showing many young children all over the world
How maths and balloons can be cool.
Once upon a time this girl called Bubblz
Just didn't know what she could be,
But now she is the funniest mathematical clown
That anyone could ever see.

# FROM THE SHEET
# TO THE STREET

David had a great idea,
That idea stayed with him all day,
That idea would not go away,
That idea grew and grew.

He thought about his great idea,
The idea just got greater,
He put it on a sheet of paper
In words, with drawings too.

David shared his big idea
With a big strong builder,
An interior designer,
And a man who had some land.

They all liked this great idea,
The day was bright and sunny
When the bank gave them some money
For the idea they had planned.

David looked at his idea,
And made it even better,
He wrote his friends a letter
To show them what he'd done.

The time had come for this idea,
So they called the builders in.
With long ladders and scaffolding,
The work had now begun.

David watched as his idea
Began to become real
With bricks and glass and steel,
And now it is complete.

David is proud of his idea,
David is an Architect.
And his building is now erect
On a busy London street.

# DAVID is an ARCHITECT

David Adjaye was born in Dar es Salaam in Tanzania, where his father was a Ghanaian diplomat, and went to school and college in London. As a child, he wanted to be a pilot. But when he was 16, his Art and Technology teacher inspired him to look towards architecture as a possible career. His parents were not keen. As they did not have any architect friends, they felt they were not able to help him. But David was determined and he did become an architect after studying hard. He thinks that children are using architecture when they imagine boxes to be houses. He enjoys his job, as it allows him to use space to improve people's lives.

# Ajmer is a Lollypop Man

**Ajmer Singh Sahota** has been a lollypop man for six years, and he cycles to work. He likes the work and life balance that the job gives him. He is on duty at the start and finish of school, as well as during the lunch break, helping children and parents cross the road safely to and from school. He says that some motorists are impolite and sometimes dangerous, when they stop too suddenly and too close to the children crossing the road. Some parents even drive on to no-entry roads to drop their children off for school. Ajmer just wants to help to keep children safe.

# Lollypop stops

He doesn't sell you lollypops
Or any other sweets,
He just takes his big lollypop
To help you cross the streets.
When he walks into the road
Raising his lollypop,
Every car that is in sight
Simply has to stop.

When you're on the way to school
You'll find him on the street,
His lollypop is made of steel
And not the sort you eat.
Even when it's dinner time
You will find him there,
Making sure that all the drivers
On the street take care.

He cares about the drivers,
He cares about the kids,
He wants to make the roads so safe
That cars don't have to skid.
When he is on duty
The law says he's the boss,
But if they're well behaved
He'll let grown-ups and doggies cross.

So those are his duties,
He will take care of you.
If you're coming or you're going
You must respect him too,
And then when you grow up one day
And you're driving around,
If you see the lollypop
Remember to slow down.

# Anthony is an Illustrator

**Anthony Browne** is a children's book illustrator whose picture books are published all over the world.
As a child he wanted to be a cartoonist, a journalist or a boxer. He learnt boxing from his dad. He feels he was destined to be an illustrator, though. He has written a series of books featuring gorillas. Once a school television programme got him to go into a cage with a gorilla, who bit him. He was not angry with the gorilla; it only made him realise that gorillas in the zoo feel like people in prison. He draws and writes about animals to show how sensitive and intelligent they are. He thinks picture books are important for the education of feelings.

# Chimps and Gorillas

He can draw mountains, and fountains, and clouds,
But he loves drawing chimps and gorillas,
He can draw football fans shouting out loud
And he can draw pink caterpillars.
He can draw elephants, big fish and birds,
He can draw otters or buffalo herds,
He can draw things that are really absurd,
But he loves drawing chimps and gorillas.

He can write stories that give you a thrill,
But he loves drawing chimps and gorillas,
Some of his stories will make you just chill
But most of his stories are thrillers.
He can draw small giraffes and giant ants,
He can because he has such confidence,
Some of his animals even wear pants,
But he loves drawing chimps and gorillas.

He has lots of ideas that live in his head,
But he loves drawing chimps and gorillas,
He dreams of stories with pictures in bed
And he sleeps with two extra soft pillows.
He has been known to draw colourful skies,
He has been known to draw quite tasty pies,
He even drew the three bears in disguise,
But he loves drawing chimps and gorillas.

He said in the future he'll draw lots of things,
But he loves drawing chimps and gorillas,
He said no one knows what the future will bring,
He could be a boxer or a miller.
If that ever happens he'll make a nice bun,
But for the time being he's just having fun,
He'll draw anything and he's glad when it's done,
But he loves drawing chimps and gorillas.

# TAKING CARE OF HISTORY

The Natural History Museum
Is where he spends his days,
Talking to the children there
And making up displays.
He does have his own children,
He even has a wife,
But he's been a Biologist
For most of his long life.

The history of all living things
Is always on his mind,
The history of all animals
And the history of mankind.
So go to his museum
And you will learn for sure,
And you will have the chance to see
A great big dinosaur.

Frogs and birds and butterflies
Are always on display,
They even have computers,
You can learn as you play.
So everyone is welcome,
That means teachers too,
Actually that means anyone,
Including me and you.

The Natural History Museum,
You could call it his office,
Many of the things you see there
Will really make you speechless.
He takes care of the visitors,
He does his job with pride,
Yes, he takes care of the building
And everything inside.

# Mike is a ZOOLOGIST

**Dr Michael Dixon**, Director of the Natural History Museum, trained as a zoologist. As a child he found nature and science fascinating and wanted to do a job that would combine the two. Before coming to the Natural History Museum he looked after the London and Whipsnade zoos. He enjoys working here because one and a half million children each year visit the Museum with their families or their school. He is overjoyed to see the look of wonder on their faces as they explore the diversity of the natural world. He believes that it is the Museum's role to inspire the next generation to care for the natural world, and to encourage children to see a career in science as a realistic and worthwhile ambition.

# Julia is a Shopkeeper

**Julia Topliss** has worked in the village shop for nine years and she really loves her job. She sells newspapers, magazines, groceries, sweets, stamps and envelopes – and lots more.

Julia says the best part of her job is seeing the village children every day, and watching them grow up. They come to the shop after school, and buy fruit chews, lollipops or Ice Pols! They are lovely, and they make her laugh. She knows everyone in the village and is popular because when she's working she is always smiling. She says it's because people are very funny.

The village is lucky because the shop is also the Post Office, and some other village post offices are being closed down. The shop is important because many people come there for advice or a chat. For some older people who live alone, it is one of the few times they get to talk to someone.

Julia spends all her spare time with her grandchildren, Chloe and Lexanne.

# The Sweeter Shopkeeper

Kids come in for sticky toffee,
Kids come in for mints and cake,
Adults come to buy some coffee,
Kids like things that just taste great.
Kids come in for cones and ices,
Some kids really take a while,
Kids come in asking for prices
And Julia serves them with a smile.

Kids come in for chewing gums
And other sticky chewy bits,
Some kids come in with their mums
Who buy them packs of crispy crisps.
Some kids come and buy some pears,
Some have walked more than a mile,
Some come in to buy éclairs
And Julia serves them with a smile.

Some adults will buy newspapers,
Many talk about the weather,
Kids and adults will do capers,
Lots of kids come in together.
Some kids will buy chocolate mousse,
Making every trip worthwhile,
Healthy kids buy fruit and juice
So Julia serves them with a smile.

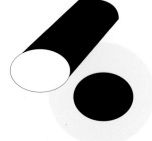

What Julia really likes the most
Is seeing people every day,
Even when they come for post
She smiles and problems go away.
Some kids come in to buy fruit chews,
Some stylish ladies come in style,
Some just come in to hear the news,
Still Julia serves them with a smile.

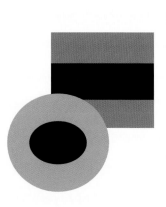
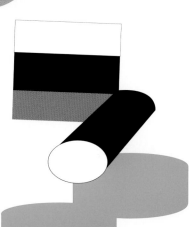

# David is a Farmer

**David Jacks** farms 1300 acres, and the farm has been in his family for over 100 years. He only does arable farming, a which means he has no animals on the farm, but grows things such as daffodils, tulips, onions, potatoes, sugar beet, beans, cauliflowers, cabbages and peas.

David first drove a tractor when he was six. In those days lots of young boys and girls worked on farms. He went to a comprehensive school, and then on to an agricultural college.

Sometimes he has to start work at 6am, and sometimes he can work until 10pm. When there is not much work to do and crops are growing he can have as few as 20 people working for him, but when it is busy and the crops have to be taken in and new crops planted, he may have over 200 workers. He tries to create jobs for local people, but many local people don't like working on farms, so most of his workers are from abroad, mainly Eastern Europe.

Most of his land is used for farming, but he has left some land to create a small forest so that wildlife can live there in peace.

# A Charmer of a Farmer

He rises with the morning sun
When the day has just begun,
Many folk would not be fed
If farmer David stayed in bed.
And very soon he's on the land
With his workers who lend a hand,
They all work these early hours
So we can have our cauliflowers.

At other times he's sowing seeds
To grow the food the nation needs,
He plants the seeds and waits a while
And soon the wheat grows from the soil.
Then when the wheat is dry and brown
In his tractor he cuts it down,
The wheat is then stored in a shed
So we can have our daily bread.

He grows leeks, beans, and potatoes
Green cabbages and tomatoes,
Part of his land is growing trees
And there you'll find some birds and bees.
His onions are very spicy
His runner beans are growing nicely,
He does this work so happily
So we can have our broccoli.

There would not be a single chip
If farmers did not do their bit,
Without them who knows where we'd be,
We really would be so hungry.
So everyone should understand
That farmer David works the land
For vegetables and sugar beet
So we can have nice things to eat.

# Shami is a Lawyer

**Shami Chakrabarti** wanted to be a lawyer when she was a child. She remembers having a conversation with her father when she was a small child about what punishment should be given to criminals. Her father told her that sometimes things are not simple and the people who are sent to jail are later found not to be guilty. That got Shami thinking about justice and how important it is to be certain of the situation before punishing someone.

Shami studied Law at the London School of Economics, where Law is studied not as a means of earning a lot of money but as a way of thinking about justice and the rights of the individual. She decided to devote her life to championing the cause of those who do not have a voice.

# Fights for Rights

She studied the law of the land,
That's how she came to understand
That everyone should have their human rights.
When others suffered she did too,
So she knew what she had to do.
She had to use some peaceful ways to fight.

Children should be treated fair,
That means children everywhere,
And Shami wants to make sure this is so.
Girls and boys should all be equal,
Equal rights for all the people,
And citizens should have the right to know.

We all have the right to walk,
We all have the right to talk,
And we have the right to get an education.
We all have the right to sing,
Rights are such important things
If you want to live in any nation.

Rights for the young,
Rights for the old,
Rights for the shy,
Rights for the bold,
Nobody should bully you,
Shami knows that this is true.
Rights for women,
Rights for men,
Rights for us,
Rights for them.
When people think their rights have gone
She fights for rights for everyone.

RIGHTS
FOR
EVERYONE

A huge thank you to everyone in the book
who gave their time so generously, to Janetta and Judith
for sharing my enthusiasm and to my family
for their support and sustenance – PD

JANETTA OTTER-BARRY BOOKS

*When I Grow Up* copyright © Frances Lincoln Limited 2011
Text copyright © Benjamin Zephaniah 2011
Photographs copyright © Prodeepta Das 2011
First published in Great Britain in 2011 and in the USA in 2012 by
Frances Lincoln Children's Books, 4 Torriano Mews,
Torriano Avenue, London NW5 2RZ
www.franceslincoln.com

A catalogue record for this book is available from the British Library.

ISBN 978-1-84780-059-6

Printed in Singapore by
Tien Wah Press (Pte) Ltd. in May 2011

1 3 5 7 9 8 6 4 2